IMAGES
of Rail

STEAM RAILROADS
OF NORTHERN IOWA AND
SOUTHERN MINNESOTA

This L2b steam locomotive on the Chicago, Milwaukee, St. Paul & Pacific Railroad in 1941 is shown at Marquette, Iowa. Engine No. 467 was on standby on a leisurely Sunday afternoon awaiting assignment on a heavy freight train heading to Mason City, Iowa. (Courtesy of Harold K. Vollrath.)

ON THE COVER: This is a Chicago, Rock Island & Pacific Railroad high-speed passenger steam engine used between Des Moines, Iowa, and Minneapolis, Minnesota, in the 1940s and early 1950s. These locomotives were extremely fast and capable of speeds of 100–110 miles per hour. These engines were specifically balanced for high-speed running in Silvis, Illinois. Here they were put on a slip track, and the spinning wheels were photographed with a high-speed motion picture camera. The spinning wheels could be photographed with stop-motion so that the master mechanic could analyze wheel balance. Correction weights could be later added to specific wheel locations to remove any imbalance. (Courtesy of the Charles Winters Collection.)

IMAGES
of Rail

STEAM RAILROADS
OF NORTHERN IOWA AND
SOUTHERN MINNESOTA

Jim Angel and Ashley Mantooth

ARCADIA
PUBLISHING

Copyright © 2019 by Jim Angel and Ashley Mantooth
ISBN 978-1-4671-0288-9

Published by Arcadia Publishing
Charleston, South Carolina

Library of Congress Control Number: 2018959295

For all general information, please contact Arcadia Publishing:
Telephone 843-853-2070
Fax 843-853-0044
E-mail sales@arcadiapublishing.com
For customer service and orders:
Toll-Free 1-888-313-2665

Visit us on the Internet at www.arcadiapublishing.com

To Jim's daughter and Ashley's aunt, Cathy Angel Cline,
whose encouragement has made all the difference

CONTENTS

ACKNOWLEDGMENTS

We would like to thank the following people for their contributions: James L. Rueber for his willingness to share his photograph collection, which made much of this book possible; Karen Bowen and the Mason City Public Library; Jim's late dear friend Safford Lock and the many images he provided from his personal collection; the Charles Winters Collection; the Cecil Cook Collection; Elwin Musser, photographer for the *Mason City Globe Gazette*; Jim's close friend Art Holtman; Gayle Ecklund from the Milwaukee Public Library; curator Nick Fry for the John W. Barringer III Collection at the National Railroad Library in St. Louis, Missouri; and the Chicago & North Western Historical Society.

All images used in this book come from the personal collection of Jim Angel unless otherwise noted.

INTRODUCTION

Let me tell you what it was like to run and fire a steam engine while working on the railroad. In 1953, I was hired by the Chicago, Milwaukee, St. Paul & Pacific Railroad, generally known as the Milwaukee Road by employees. The traveling engineer on the Iowa Dakota Division, Ralph Replogle, called me into his office in the huge roundhouse at Mason City, Iowa, to discuss the open position. After talking a while to see if I was serious, he handed me technical documents on the locomotives, both steam and diesel. I was then sent to the company physician for a check-up. Eye tests were especially critical for men working on the railroad. I underwent two color vision tests; the first was the Ichihara test, and the second was the yarn test. The Ichihara test consisted of multiple colored dots and tested for red-green color blindness. If you were color blind, you would be able to see different numbers than a person who was not color blind. The yarn test comprised hundreds of variously colored strands of wool yarn placed in a small container and covered by a wooden tab. With the yarn covered up, I was asked to pull out all of the red, then green, then blue, then yellow yarns. A count was made of what you selected, and you passed or failed based on the amount of correct colors pulled. I am sure after 65 years this old yarn testing method is obsolete. However, color discernment is still very important today, as color signaling continues to be used on the railroad.

After passing all the tests, I was set up for my first training, or what was commonly called a student trip, on a steam locomotive. I drove my old 1931 Ford Model A down to the roundhouse on a bitter cold November day. The roundhouse foreman, Paul Hurley, met me at the door and asked if I had a pair of goggles. I said "no," and he handed me a pair. He took me into the engineer's crew room, where crewmembers awaited their runs. All the men in the room were dressed in overalls, engineer caps, jackets, and neckerchiefs. Neckerchiefs prevented the hot cinders from burning the back of your neck. An engineer, Foster Merritt, saw me and said, "Come over here, kid!" I later learned that most engineers had nicknames given to them by other employees; over the years from then on, I was called "Kid" rather than my given name. I then met the fireman, Leonard Dean, a very likable man who took good care of me. I was shown a board that had the rules of the day. These rules were to be read before each trip. I was also shown the Interstate Commerce Commission (ICC) reports on locomotive boiler explosions (Congress abolished this regulatory department in 1995). As far as I know, no one ever survived a boiler explosion of a locomotive. It is important to note that safety was a top priority each day.

I went out with the fireman to our waiting locomotive, an L2b heavy freight engine. This was a stoker-fired engine, so I was taught how to use a scoop shovel to lay coal into several critical areas in the firebox to make the engine steam better. I was taught to operate the injectors, which keep the boiler filled to the necessary water level when standing and when running. The level was monitored by watching the water glass to ensure a safe amount of water was in the boiler at all times. Next, I was shown where the supply of waste was kept. Waste was made out of leftover threads and scraps from the big textile mills and was bundled together and used for keeping all of the gauges clean and for a number of other housekeeping chores. This material was used by all railroads in all engines and cabooses for general cleaning. Waste was also soaked in oil and used in the journal box bearings on all railroad cars to lubricate the wheel bearings. I was also shown how to use the squirt hose, which took super-heated water directly out of the boiler, to clean the floor of the cab, the seats, and the back head of the boiler before we moved the engine. We were almost ready to move our engine to the train. I was shown how to use the blower, which would keep the smoke up for visibility. The engineer opened the cylinder cocks before we moved to the train. This prevented water from collecting in the steam cylinders. Water is incompressible, and if not removed from the steam cylinders, it could blow the cylinder heads off, and this could disable the engine. We moved to the train—the stoker was running, the blower was on, and the steam pressure was standing at 200 pounds per square inch. The injector was turned on to keep the water flowing from the tender into the boiler as we carefully watched the water glass to assure safety.

Leaving town on a steam locomotive was not like driving away in an automobile, like driving a bus, or even like running a diesel locomotive—on a steam engine, it was an event. Foster Merritt, the engineer, hollered, "Are we ready?" and we replied with an affirmative hand wave. The engineer then gave one blast of the whistle to indicate he was going to make an air test. He operated the handle to draw off 15 pounds per square inch of air brake pressure, while the crew in the caboose watched its air pressure gauge also. If the crew's air gauge showed no loss of pressure other than the test reduction, the conductor would give a high ball signal to the engineer. The engineer opened the throttle and the engine stalled, Foster backed up to take slack, and he pushed the reverse lever forward. With two blasts of the whistle, we were off!

When finally moving with our train, the blower was on to lift the smoke out of the stack. The steam injector was on to force water into the boiler and maintain a safe water level of about three inches in the water glass. A steam pop-off valve was sounding, and the engine exhaust was roaring. At that point, no conversation was possible because of the great noise. We had to cross the tracks of the Minneapolis & St. Louis Railway. The firemen looked to the left and hollered "all clear" to the engineer. The engineer watched to the right and answered with the same reply. Visibility was limited by the boiler, so we had to work together to makes sure no other trains were coming from the north or south. The engineer then widened out on the throttle, and we accelerated to track speed. Steam engines were rough riding. With each thrust of the pistons, the engine cab developed strong lateral motion, and you had to hang on tight. We had to make a long sweeping curve to the left before we reached the Chicago, Rock Island & Pacific Railroad crossing. The engineer could not see this crossing because of the long boiler, so he was on the lookout for our hand signal, which would tell him if we should stop or proceed. The crossing had a tall signal with a metal cross arm operated by a telegrapher inside the depot who could see both directions. The signal would be horizontal with a red light if a Rock Island train was in the block. If there was not another train coming, the cross arm would be vertical with a green light showing. Green lights indicated it was safe to proceed, and we would holler "high green" to the engineer, meaning we could proceed safely at track speed. A "high green" was hollered back from the engineer to affirm the signal.

Firing an engine at speed meant keeping an eye on the condition of the fire. We would open the fire door, using the back side of the shovel to block the glare, and look in to see if the fire was burning level. If the fire showed extreme bright spots, even though the stoker was running fine, the fireman would shovel in big scoops of coal to cover them. These spots meant the fire was too thin and cold air was coming up through them. If this was not addressed by the fireman, the cold air would cool the engine down and could reduce boiler steam pressure. Firing an engine was a constant battle to maintain proper engine performance. You had to watch the fire, watch the steam pressure and maintain 200 pounds per square inch, watch the smoke to maintain a hazy grey color for best coal consumption, and watch your side of the train for any problems. Trains of this era did not have roller bearings; instead, the journal bearings were made of Babbitt alloy metal covered with oily waste. These bearings would sometimes run hot or catch fire, and this was called a hot box. You had to be on the lookout for signs of heat or fire. At night, you would look over the train and call out to the engineer "all black." In the daytime, you would do the same but call out "all blue" if there were no signs of heat or fire. This was done on every train. Each run was an adventure. Firemen were responsible for filling the engine tender with coal and water during each trip, winter or summer, at every coal and water stop along the way. We also learned about running the locomotives under the guidance of the engineer.

Running these great machines was a fascinating experience. I will never forget the melancholy sound of a steam whistle on a warm summer evening. For me, it has always invoked feelings of loneliness, sadness, faraway places, and the excitement of travel across our great nation. My passion for steam railroads has inspired me to share this collaboration of sights and sounds. I hope these photographs give a broader understanding of the intricacies of steam engines, what it took to operate these giant locomotives, the obstacles and dangers faced by the engine crews, and the rich history surrounding Northern Iowa and Southern Minnesota through the end of a golden era.

—Jim Angel

One

STEAM ENGINE OPERATIONS

This photograph shows a Milwaukee Road L2b engine at Marquette, Iowa, just out of the shops, where it has undergone a complete rebuild. This is one type of locomotive the author worked on while learning to fire a steam engine on the Iowa Dakota Division. This photograph of engine No. 409 was taken in 1953. The engine was built in 1921. (Courtesy of Milwaukee Public Library.)

Running steam locomotives year-round in the Midwest was quite an operation. The large building, called a coal chute, emptied railroad cars as they passed through. Once unloaded, the coal was lifted up to the top of the chute and emptied into storage bins. Firemen would then drop the coal down the metal chute shown into the engine tenders. The large water tank was used for water treatment. Underground pipes carried the water to smaller standpipes, where firemen could fill the locomotive water tenders. The slender tower shown beyond the coal chute contained dry sand, which was used to fill the sand domes on the top of the engines. Engineers would trickle sand on the rails in front or behind the driving wheels to add traction in times of wet or slippery conditions.

Chicago Great Western engine No. 914 is shown at the coal chute in Mason City, Iowa, ready to take coal. The fireman, who is obscured by the steam, is standing on the tender and is preparing to pull the coal chute down. Lowering the metal chute allows the coal to flow down into the engine tender. Steam engines had to be changed at Clarion, Iowa, and Hayfield, Minnesota. This hand-fired steam engine is pulling a daily passenger train called the *Omaha Express* from Minneapolis, Minnesota, to Omaha, Nebraska.

Engine No. 914 is preparing to leave the coal chute and will move to the water tower before it can proceed to the passenger depot. The coal chute will remain in the upright position, as shown between the steam and smoke, until the next engine arrives to receive coal.

A Chicago & North Western JS freight engine is shown alongside the roundhouse at Mason City, Iowa. This is not a high-quality photograph, but it shows the large pile of wood that would be used for firing up the engine. The firemen would shovel coal on the bare grates in the firebox, and then a wheelbarrow full of wood would be thrown on top of the coal. Finally, a large handful of oily waste, comprising leftover threads and fibers purchased from textile mills, was lit and thrown on the wood.

This photograph shows the inside of the firebox of a JS-class engine. The fire is ready for lighting, with a bed of coals on the grates and kindling wood covering the coal. The flue's large pipes are visible running the length of the boiler. To start the fire, a fireman would soak a handful of waste in oil, light the fibers, then throw the bundle on the wood. All railroads used waste for cleaning and firing purposes.

Hostler John Ficken is moving this R1-class locomotive, engine No. 1403, into position so that the side rods can be greased. Every 100 to 150 miles, the steam engines had to stop for care and maintenance. The old bed of fire, perhaps three feet deep, had to be shaken down on one side of the firebox and removed from the engine. Twelve-foot-long fire rakes were then used to rake hot coals from the full side of the firebox to the empty side, and more coal was shoveled in to rebuild a fire bed about five to six inches deep. This process was then repeated for the other side of the firebox. This job took a strong, skilled man about one hour to complete. Another man would then use a high-pressure grease gun to pump hard grease into all of the rods on both sides of the engine. The grease used here was so hard that one could carry a five-inch grease stick without getting one's hands dirty. These engines were used for lightweight freight trains and were hand-fired. They used the Stephenson valve gear, which required two sloping cylinders. This put all of the valve gear between the wheels, with none of it on the outside of the driving wheels, making it more difficult to maintain.

These photographs depict the cab of engine No. 2504 in 1953. The fireman's side is shown on the left and the engineer's side on the right. The left side shows the valves that operate the steam-powered stoker so that the fireman does not have to hand-fire the engine, along with the steam pressure and stoker gauges. The engineer would also use the long-necked oil can, shown in center-left, and the engine oil can, shown at center. The valve oil can, on the far right, would be used to fill the automatic oiler.

Milwaukee Road L2b-class engine No. 436 is preparing to take on coal at the Tama, Iowa, coal chute. This chute was capable of fueling an engine on either set of tracks. The fireman would move the chute in order to take coal for the engine he was on. This was part of the double track on the Chicago, Milwaukee, St. Paul & Pacific Railroad. (Courtesy of James L. Rueber.)

This Chicago & North Western switch engine, No. 2135, is heading toward the coal chute on a quiet Sunday morning in Mason City, Iowa. This is an M2-class switch engine preparing for Monday operations, when it could be switching in the Mason yard or taking trips to the Northwestern States Portland Cement Company.

Engine No. 2135 is shown near the Chicago & North Western roundhouse. Hostlers were railroad engineers who moved locomotives in and out of service facilities. Hostler John Ficken and his two sons are posing for a picture.

This photograph shows the front of the depot of the Rock Island and Chicago Great Western Railroads at Mason City, Iowa. The water tank is showing two spouts in the upright position. A passenger train is seen heading north from the depot after dropping off and picking up passengers and mail.

The Chicago Great Western water tank is being removed from service in Mason City, Iowa, in 1950. The spouts were used to feed the steam engines at one time. The numbering on this tank shows that it could hold 16 feet of water. Tanks being pulled down, usually by an engine, indicated the end of steam.

This is a close-up of a fireman on engine No. 912 taking water. The employee timetable is shown in his back pocket. Employee timetables were not the same as passenger timetables. Employee timetables told firemen where the coal chutes and water towers were located. They gave important information, such as what speeds were allowed. Everything in the employee timetable gave direction for the engine crew and the conductor for daily operations. Passenger timetables told the arrival and departure times for passenger trains. These were usually printed and updated on a quarterly basis.

A fireman is shown taking water on for engine No. 912's boiler on this passenger train in Mason City, Iowa. He is using the water tank's spout to fill the tender. After the engine is filled with coal, it needs to be filled with water. The passenger train will then move south to take on passengers at the joint depot used by the Chicago Great Western and the Chicago, Rock Island & Pacific Railroads. The train will continue on to Fort Dodge, Iowa, and Omaha, Nebraska.

During the 1930s, many camera clubs were started by people interested in photography as smaller and better cameras using 35-millimeter film became popular. This photograph of engine No. 802 was taken in 1937 on the Milwaukee Road at Mason City, Iowa, during the changing of engines. Engines were changed and maintained about every 100 miles to clean the fires. The time exposure shows the engine popping off at 200 pounds per square inch of boiler pressure. This was a common occurrence, and it made for a spectacular night photograph. This F5 passenger engine is headed east at Mason City, Iowa, pulling the passenger train named *The Sioux*. These engines had stokers, and they were fast. (Courtesy of Art Holtman.)

This shows the last car of the Milwaukee Road passenger train No. 22, *The Sioux*, leaving Mason City, Iowa. It is pulled by engine No. 802. Mason City was an engine change point. Engine No. 802 was put on this train for the run to Marquette, Iowa. This is a time exposure of the last car, and the tail sign indicates its name. After leaving Marquette, it will continue on to Chicago, Illinois. (Courtesy Art of Holtman.)

Milwaukee Road L2b-class engine No. 518 is stopped at the Mason City, Iowa, roundhouse and water tanks. The engineer is discussing a main rod bearing that is running warm. The traveling engineer is listening, and a decision will be made as to whether the engine can proceed to the train or if it will have to go into the roundhouse for work. (Courtesy of Milwaukee Public Library.)

M2-class switch engine No. 2135 is shown behind the legs of the sand tower. The long rakes leaning against the tower will be used for cleaning the fires. The tower stores sand that can be spread on the tracks by the engineer during inclement weather. (Courtesy of Safford Lock.)

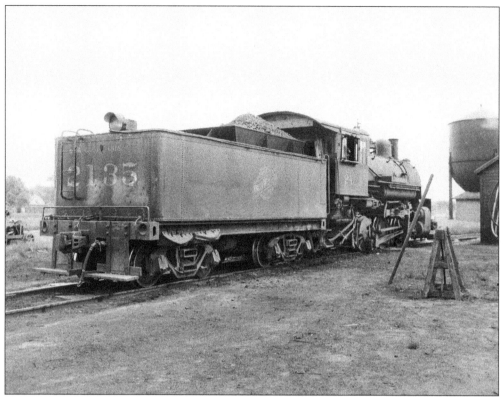

Switch engine No. 2135 is shown with frogs hanging over the rear tender wheels. Frogs are heavy devices that can lifted off of the engine to assist in a derailment. One or two men could place the frogs ahead or behind a pair of derailed wheels, and the engine would pull the car back on the track.

The Chicago Great Western coal chute is shown in the background. The picture was taken north of the shared depot in Mason City, Iowa. There are 1930s-era automobiles parked at the section house on the left. The smoke is coming from Chicago Great Western steam switch engine No. 471, which is being fired up for the daily switching duties. (Courtesy of Art Holtman.)

This coal chute was used by the Chicago & North Western Railroad at Mason City, Iowa. This chute was in use until dieselization occurred in 1956. Parts of the chute are shown scattered in the foreground as it is being torn down. (Courtesy of James L. Rueber.)

This photograph at Mason City, Iowa, shows the tower of the Chicago Great Western interlocking plant system. This system allows three mainline railroads to cross one another safely at grade level. These railroads are the Chicago Great Western, the Chicago & North Western, and the Chicago, Rock Island & Pacific. If a Chicago Great Western train is heading north from Mason City to Minneapolis, the engineer will see a semaphore signal post on the right side of the track. The signal tells the engineer to stop when both a red light and the semaphore blade are in the horizontal stop position. The engineer will stop his train and give one long blast of his whistle to get permission from the tower to cross. If the tower men do not see trains approaching from the other railroads, they will pull large levers to give a stop signal to the intersecting tracks. After the other railroads are blocked, the stop signal to the Chicago Great Western train will be cleared, and the engineer can proceed with his train. The interlocking system prevents any of the other railroads from crossing any other tracks, allowing safe passage for all the railroads. (Courtesy of Art Holtman.)

Two

THE HEIGHT OF STEAM LOCOMOTIVES

Steam switch engines, such as this M2, were very powerful. They could pull up to twenty 100-ton carloads of cement out of the two Mason City, Iowa, cement plants. The cement was then put on trains going to other cities across Iowa and Minnesota. The crewmen are pictured at the Chicago & North Western yard in Mason City; from left to right are fireman Harry Vining, engineer John Christianson, and switchmen Ray Gillam, Harry Preston, and Clyde Hathaway.

This very rare picture shows a Shay steam engine owned by the North Western States Portland Cement Plant. It has three vertical cylinders on the side that drive a crankshaft connected via gear to the wheels. These little engines were slow but powerful. They pulled cars of lime, rock, and clay from the cement plant quarries. This engine was taken out of service and replaced by a fleet of giant dump trucks at the end of World War II. (Courtesy of Art Holtman.)

Engine No. 3016 was one of the largest steam engines operated on the Chicago & North Western Railway. These huge machines were originally built in 1930 as H-class engines. They were dual-service engines, as they could handle high-speed freight trains and could also pull passenger trains up to 90 miles per hour. Here, the engine men are examining the valve gear at Belle Plaine, Iowa, to ensure a safe run. (Courtesy of James L. Rueber.)

Passenger engine No. 2904 of the Chicago & North Western Railway is shown at Boone, Iowa, pulling a fast passenger and mail train. Note that this engine has no spokes on the 81-inch-diameter engine drive wheels. These wheels were called Boxpok drive wheels. They were carefully counterbalanced for smooth running at 100 miles per hour.

Engine No. 399 is a D-class engine of the Chicago & North Western Railway. These engines were built in the 1900s. The drive wheels were extremely tall and measured around 81 inches in diameter. These engines pulled the fast mail trains and could easily exceed 100 miles per hour. (Courtesy of James L. Rueber.)

Two engine men pose for a picture in Mason City, Iowa, as this J-class engine, No. 2306, is preparing for a special occasion. It will be pulling an inspection train of Chicago & North Western officials to examine the condition of the railroads tracks from Mason City to Belle Plaine, Iowa. The engine has been cleaned up and is carrying white flags to run as extra. Extra trains were not scheduled, and the operations would be controlled by the dispatcher using train orders. This engine is still hand-fired, as it has not yet been converted to the JS class. (Courtesy of Mason City Public Library.)

Engine No. 2528 was rebuilt as a JA-class engine in 1938. Steam pressure was raised to 200 pounds per square inch, a larger water tender was applied, disc drivers were added, and improved lateral motion devices allowed the engine to run faster and smoother. This type of engine was used for fast freight service. (Courtesy of Chicago Northwestern Historical Society.)

30

This Chicago & North Western ES-class steam passenger engine No. 620 is awaiting assignment at Belle Plaine, Iowa. The left side of the engine is shown. These locomotives were shrouded to simulate a streamline effect. (Courtesy of Robert Walz.)

Here is the right side of passenger engine No. 620. These were used in fast passenger service across Iowa and Minnesota. The color scheme of these locomotives was yellow and green. They were a beautiful sight as they raced across the Midwestern landscape. (Courtesy of Robert Walz.)

Chicago & North Western engine No. 2599 was the last JS-class steam engine to operate in Mason City on the North Iowa Division. Hostler John Ficken is making the last move for the camera before killing the fire. The author took this photograph from the engineer's side of the engine during this event. These engines could pull trains up to 3,250 tons with stokers, while a man could only handle 2,500 tons. Fireman Ben Beyer was called the "Iron Fireman" because he was the only man in Mason City who could keep one of these brutes hot at 200 pounds per square inch. Hand-firing these engines was no small task.

Switch engine No. 471 of the Chicago Great Western is working at Mason City, Iowa. The Chicago Great Western roundhouse was blown down by a tornado in the early 1920s, and this engine was never sheltered indoors. Every 30 days, steam engine boilers had to be washed out, and without the necessary equipment, this engine had to be moved to the Chicago & North Western roundhouse for maintenance. This engine operated from 1940 until 1950, when the Chicago Great Western dieselized. (Courtesy of Harold K. Vollrath.)

Chicago Great Western Railroad engine No. 750, a heavy freight engine showing open cylinder cocks, is moving onto the turntable at Clarion, Iowa, on October 7, 1933. The cylinder cocks are open to remove any excess water from the steam cylinders. (Courtesy of James L. Rueber.)

Chicago Great Western Railroad engine No. 917 is photographed in Hayfield, Minnesota, on August 23, 1940. These engines were used on passenger trains from Minneapolis, Minnesota, to Omaha, Nebraska. This train stopped at the Mason City depot while en route. These engines were hand-fired. The position of the reverse gear indicates that this engine is prepared to back up. (Courtesy of James L. Rueber.)

The Chicago, Rock Island & Pacific Railroad was commonly known as the Rock Island. This large steam engine, No. 4050, belonged to the Rock Island and was photographed by the author in 1954 at Manly, Iowa. This engine was on standby protection duty in the event that one of the Rock Island's fast diesel-powered passenger trains suffered an engine failure.

This photograph shows the left side of engine No. 4050. These locomotives weighed 368 tons and were capable of speeds of 90 to 100 miles per hour. The roundhouse foreman, when questioned if these engines could make rocket speeds, replied, "Hell yes they can make rocket speed, or better, if they aren't afraid to ride her . . . and there are plenty here that ain't afraid!"

Keith Van Note was Jim Angel's best friend. He is shown by engine No. 4050. Keith had the same passion for airplanes as Jim does for trains. After this picture was taken, Keith joined the Air Force cadet program, and he rose to the rank of major in the US Air Force. He was a navigator on a C-130 cargo plane. Sadly, he was killed in an accidental collision with an F-102 Delta Dagger fighter. There were no survivors. Jim has fond memories of the two of them exploring both aircraft and locomotives over the years. Keith was buried at the Elmwood Cemetery in Mason City, Iowa, on December 15, 1972.

This photograph shows the interior view of the cab on the engineer's side of engine No. 4050. The doors on the firebox are called butterfly fire doors. They open like a butterfly spreading its wings. All of the engineer's controls are shown: brake valves, throttle, reverse gear, low water alarm, signal lights, and other indicators used by the engineer when running one of these monsters.

This is a close-up of engine No. 4050 showing the valve and steam cylinders on the left side of the locomotive. Note the vertical levers of the reversing gear and the oil pump driven by the piston valve gear. The steam piston is attached to a point called the cross head, which carries the piston back and forth. All steam engines had tires on their drive wheels. They are not rubber tires but four-inch-thick steel tires that would be replaced every 75,000 miles or so. Heat and powerful pressure were required to take them off the engine and replace them.

This close-up of the front of engine No. 4050 shows a good view of what is called the pilot. The dings and dents on the pilot are a result of many encounters with rocks, tree limbs, and debris, as well as an occasional automobile, while in motion.

This is the massive water tender of engine No. 4050. This tender carries up to 18 tons of coal and 20,000 gallons of water. All of the wheels on this locomotive and tender are roller bearing. The steam pipes at the rear of this engine are designed to connect to the passenger cars for steam heating in cold weather.

Engine No. 5043 was one of the largest steam engines that the Rock Island owned. These were often called 5000-class engines. They were immensely heavy and could only be used through Mason City, Iowa, after 1939, when all of the bridges were strengthened. (Courtesy of Charles Winters Collection.)

Engine No. 5044 of the 5000 class is preparing to back up, as the reverse levers are in this position above the main drive wheel. These massive engines weighed nearly 425 tons. (Courtesy of Charles Winters Collection.)

The Chicago, Milwaukee, St. Paul & Pacific Railroad was commonly known as the Milwaukee Road by employees. This F5-class engine, No. 810, carries white flags, as this was an extra freight train coming out of Marquette, Iowa, in 1940. This train would soon be hitting the steep hill up to Monona, Iowa. Thankfully, the fireman is on a stoker-fired engine, which makes his job much easier on the heavy grade up Monona Hill. (Courtesy of Milwaukee Public Library.)

Milwaukee Road F5-class engine No. 841 sits at Mason City, Iowa. Engines of this class were stoker-fired and were used on passenger trains and light freight trains. These were generally easy to fire and smooth riding. (Courtesy of Milwaukee Public Library.)

Milwaukee Road L2b engine No. 508 is moving east with an extra water tender. The main tender and extra tender each hold 10,000 gallons. The extra tender allowed these locomotives to skip many water stops for a faster run. These engines and tenders pulled refrigerated cars from Sioux Falls, South Dakota, to Chicago, Illinois. These trains were known to the railroad workers as the "Fast Meat Trains." Trains leaving Sioux Falls around 4:00 p.m. were to be at Western Avenue in Chicago the next morning. Stops were made in Sanborn, Mason City, and Marquette, Iowa, and a few additional stops were made in Illinois for changing out the steam engine. Engines had to have their fires cleaned and crew changes had to be made to ensure timely arrival. It was quicker for crews to change to a fresh engine versus stopping and taking time to clean the fire and do necessary maintenance. During the engine changes, the car men would also go along the train and pour hot oil into each of the journal boxes to ensure proper lubrication of the wheel bearings. (Courtesy of Milwaukee Public Library.)

Milwaukee Road L2b engine No. 406 is heading west at Postville, Iowa, after coming up Monona Hill from the Marquette, Iowa, yard. Fireman Johnny Nelson is keeping his eye on the smoke, which is very light. This indicates a very good fire, and the engine steam pressure is right on target at 200 pounds per square inch. The engineer, not seen, is Scratchy Zeller. (Courtesy of Cecil Cook Collection.)

Milwaukee Road engine No. 430 heads west past Fort Atkinson, Iowa. A clean smokestack indicates a good fire. A small steam leak of no consequence can be seen just above the left steam cylinder. Note the clean engine—this was typical of the way the Milwaukee Road maintained its engines. (Courtesy of Cecil Cook Collection.)

Engine No. 430 heads west on train No. 91, working hard while coming around the curve near Calmer, Iowa. The crewmembers are fireman Johnny Nelson and engineer Scratchy Zeller. Interestingly, two of the engine men on the Iowa Dakota Division had night blindness, which prevented them from working nights. One was Mike Kelroy, who worked the day switch engine in the Mason City yard. The other was Johnny Nelson. He typically worked trains No. 68 and No. 91 between Mason City and Marquette, Iowa, because these were mainly scheduled as day trains. (Courtesy of Cecil Cook Collection.)

Engine No. 430 is shown after being cut off from train No. 91. Engine men Zeller and Nelson are moving the engine to take coal and water on a cold day. After this, the local Calmar, Iowa, switch engine will remove some of their cars and add on additional cars. Engine No. 430 will then move back to train No. 91 and proceed west to Mason City, Iowa. (Courtesy of Cecil Cook Collection.)

Minneapolis & St. Louis engine No. 502 is pictured in Mason City, Iowa, in 1936. This engine was on standby in the event that a Doodlebug light passenger engine failed. (Courtesy of James L. Rueber.)

Switch engine No. 65 of the Minneapolis & St. Louis Railway is preparing to stop at the standpipe to take water at Mason City, Iowa, in 1936. Switch engines of the series numbered 60 to 68 were actually old road locomotives of the mogul class with a wheel arrangement of 2-6-0. The 2-6-0s had a two-wheel leading truck at the front of the locomotive that could easily follow the rough tracks when they were working at cement plants or other industrial locations around Mason City. The engines could no longer handle the big trains on the main line, but they made great switch engines while working yard service. (Courtesy of James L. Rueber.)

Engine No. 63 is at the Minneapolis & St. Louis roundhouse at Mason City, Iowa, in 1940. Bill Collins was the roundhouse foreman, and his five-year-old grandson is shown standing on the footboard of the switch engine, built in 1908 by Baldwin.

The Minneapolis & St. Louis Railway was commonly abbreviated as the M&St.L. Engine No. 410 has old slide-valve steam chests and was used on lightly trafficked branch lines. It was built in 1909 and operated until 1950. (Courtesy of James L. Rueber.)

Engine No. 311 is shown on an air-operated turntable on a lazy Sunday summer afternoon in front of the M&St.L roundhouse. This engine was built by the American Locomotive Company. This information is on the builder plate shown on the side of the smokebox. These engines showed their age, but they were meticulously cared for. (Courtesy of James L. Rueber.)

This 600-class engine, No. 604, was rebuilt at the Cedar Lake Shops in Minneapolis, Minnesota. It shows two sets of air pumps sitting on the pilot. These pumps were added to reduce the time it took to pump up the air lines on longer freight trains. These stoker-fired engines carried 200 pounds per square inch of boiler pressure. Drifting valves are shown atop the cylinders. These valves reduced the heat on the locomotive valve rings from 1,000 degrees to 600 degrees Fahrenheit when the engine was drifting or coasting down long hills. (Courtesy of Art Holtman.)

Engine No. 410 is shown double-heading an unidentified 600-class engine. Engine No. 410 is carrying the white flags of an extra (unscheduled) train. This was an old engine with slide valves built in 1909. The M&St.L had to make do with every engine it could muster, but the engines were always kept in tip-top shape. Milwaukee Road engineers always talked about the sound of the exhausts being exactly square, meaning the valve timing that controlled the steam going to the cylinders was absolutely accurate. No smoke is showing in this photograph. The crew knew they were getting their picture taken, so they did not want to show any smoke. Showing smoke might be taken as a sign of wasteful firing. (Courtesy of Safford Lock.)

Engine No. 634 is shown with several improvements, including a larger sand dome, a higher boiler pressure, an additional air pump, and non-lifting injectors, all of which led to greater engine capabilities. (Courtesy of Safford Lock.)

Minneapolis & St. Louis engine No. 616 is shown south of Mason City. The 600 class of steam locomotives were the largest engines on the road built without stokers. The M&St.L operated under severe financial difficulty for most of its existence. In 1937, the ICC, which was formed in 1910, ruled that steam engines exceeding 170,000 pounds on the driving wheels had to have stokers installed. The engines were capable of delivering more horsepower to pull heavier trains if they had stokers, which could exceed the capabilities of any fireman hand-firing an engine. This work was done by the M&St.L at the Cedar Lake Shops near Minneapolis. Engine No. 616 has a stoker applied. (Courtesy of Safford Lock.)

M&St.L engine No. 456 is shown at Mason City, Iowa. The conductor, engineer, and fireman are standing below the cab of this double-header. When they finish their discussion, they will move to their designated locations. The fireman and the engineer will climb into the cab. Once they whistle off and begin to move, the conductor will walk toward the rear of the train and be ready to get on the caboose as it goes by. Once the conductor is aboard the caboose, he will wave a high ball to the engineer, signaling "full speed ahead." (Courtesy of James L. Rueber.)

In 1943, Minneapolis & St. Louis locomotive No. 451 is photographed in the M&St.L switching yard in Mason City, Iowa. The author used to watch these engines from his grandfather's windows, which backed up to the M&St.L railroad yard. This engine is unique: there is a steam booster on the tender wheels at the rear end of the coal and water tender. This booster had two small steam cylinders driving one pair of wheels on the tender. The steam for this booster came from the locomotive's main boiler. This allowed the engine to start much heavier trains. While the booster enabled it to start a train that only a 600-class locomotive could start, it could not make the speed of a 600-class steam engine. (Courtesy of James L. Rueber.)

Switch engine No. 64 was built in 1908 and photographed in 1939 along the M&St.L roundhouse. These little engines, called moguls, were built for over-the-road freight trains. They were later modified with footboards to be used as yard switch engines. Switch men would stand on the footboards rather than walking alongside the engines. Safety rules dictated when and where men could board the footboards: one only boards a footboard if it is moving away so that if one were to fall, it would be away from the engine. The person in this photograph is unidentified but likely worked for the M&St.L. (Courtesy of James L. Rueber.)

M&St.L engine No. 471 sits abandoned in 1966 at Chaska, Minnesota. This engine is the same class as engine No. 457, which has been preserved at Mason City, Iowa. No. 471 worked at the American Crystal Sugar plant near Chaska for an estimated four years. Scavengers picked it over after it was shoved into the weeds, where it sat rusting away for about a dozen years.

Three

COMPLICATIONS OF THE MIDWEST LANDSCAPE

Engine No. 2504, a Chicago & North Western JA-class freight engine, stands on the electric turntable in Mason City, Iowa, before it heads to the roundhouse for service. Winters were long and harsh for railroad men in Northern Iowa. Foot warmers were eventually added to the engineer's side of the cab to combat the bitter cold temperatures. Steam was taken from the boiler and piped to heating coils in the floor to provide warmth for the engineer's feet.

This is the cab view of JA steam locomotive No. 2504 at Mason City, Iowa, on the ready track preparing to take a train from Mason City to Belle Plaine, Iowa. Steam locomotives did not have heating or cooling in the engine cabs. Winter warmth came off the boiler, and the canvas curtains at the back of the engine cab would be pulled closed to keep out the bitter cold. Windows could be opened and the canvas could be removed during the summer to keep the engineers cool.

Two heavy Illinois Central steam locomotives are stuck in the snow west of Fort Dodge, Iowa, in the blizzard of 1936. Extreme weather was one of the hardest obstacles that the railroad faced during the blizzard of 1936. This snowplow was no match for the storm, hence the immobility of these engines.

The locomotives have been blown down so that the boiler water would not freeze if they remained stuck in the snow for some time. Railroad crew rules dictate two cabooses, each requiring five men on board. A coal-burning potbelly stove in each ensured the men could weather any storm when stuck in inclement weather.

Smoke is billowing from the smokestacks of the rescue engines attempting to free these snow-blocked locomotives. Once freed, the engines will be pulled back to the roundhouse at Fort Dodge, Iowa, where men can work on them in warmer conditions.

Two heavy Illinois Central steam locomotives are stuck in deep snow—up to 15 feet—near Fort Dodge, Iowa, in 1936. This year was considered to have the most severe snow storms in Iowa's history. These engines had to have their boilers blown down to remove the water so that it did not freeze during the two days they were stuck in the snowdrift. This weather record continued into the 1950s.

This photograph should be easy to date. A brand-new 1936 four-door V8 Ford sedan is being used by the road master and staff on the Milwaukee Road to inspect rails and roadbeds. The tires are sitting on the rails, and there is a small flange behind the front tires so that the car can drive these rails. Inspection cars made good sense—most side roads in Iowa were gravel, making it hard to inspect the track closely. Automobile wheels had a width of 4 feet, 8.5 inches, the same as railroad car wheels, so they could easily drive along the rails. For safety, these cars operated like an extra, which had no scheduled time table. They operated via train orders from a dispatcher.

This photograph shows one of the Chicago, Rock Island & Pacific Railroad snowplows. These snowplows were heavily weighted, up to approximately 100 tons. They were pushed by steam engines through snow up to 12 feet deep. These plows could reach speeds of 50 to 60 miles per hour, which allowed them to plow through the deep snowdrifts. With the harsh winters in Northern Iowa and Southern Minnesota, this type of snowplow was frequently called upon. All railroads had similar snowplows that were used on their individual tracks.

This photograph is included to show the city water tank at Clear Lake, Iowa. It is covered in ice, which was normal in the bitterly cold winters of Northern Iowa.

Chicago Great Western trackmen are replacing railroad ties just north of Ninth Street, NW, in Mason City, Iowa, on a cold winter day. Heavy maintenance of the railbed, such as replacing ties, had to be done year-round.

The Chicago Great Western Railroad crossing at Mason City, Iowa, is shown after a heavy snowstorm. The crossing watchman's house is on the right. Before the advent of electric crossing signals at First Street, NW, a watchman was stationed in the house, and it was equipped with a potbelly coal stove to provide warmth. When a train whistled, the watchman would come out carrying an old stop-or-go sign so that he could warn automobile traffic of an oncoming train. (Courtesy of Elwin Musser.)

Most of the Chicago Great Western watchmen were roundhouse mechanics or boilermakers who had lost an eye in a job-related accident. Safety glasses were not in use in those days. The Chicago Great Western Railroad would keep these men on the job as crossing guards so that they could still make a few dollars. (Courtesy of Elwin Musser.)

Chicago & North Western Railroad JS-class engine No. 2437 is shown after the blizzard of 1949. The steam engine was pushing a snowplow at about 50 miles per hour in Fairmont, Minnesota. The snowplow derailed and turned sideways on the track, then was struck by the engine. The engineer, Karl Geiler, and the other crewmembers were not injured. The locomotive was pulled back to Mason City, Iowa, where this photograph was taken, and the engine was ultimately scrapped.

The engine plate of No. 2437 was removed from the wrecked JS-class engine. The author has kept this plate for many years to serves as a memento of the great era of steam.

The left side of engine No. 2437 is shown from inside the engine cab. This view is looking out from the fireman's front window down along the boiler. The engine is sitting in the yard at Mason City, Iowa.

Minneapolis & St. Louis engines No. 229 and No. 623 are shown double-heading at Waterville, Minnesota, in 1942. This extra is shown with white flags waving on a bitterly cold winter day. Railroad cars were especially hard to pull in the cold weather. Friction bearings were used on all freight cars during this era. Roller bearings did not appear on railroad freight cars until about 1957, and they become much easier to pull. (Courtesy of Harold K. Vollrath.)

Electric locative No. 61 of the Iowa Terminal Railroad is plowing heavy snow west of Mason City, Iowa, in 1959. The snowplow is heading west along Highway 106.

Engine No. 61 is stalled in the deep snow. The engine is pushing snow up to 10 feet deep and simply does not have enough power to push through. It will back up about 1,000 feet and go forward again at full power. This process will be repeated until the engine breaks through the snow.

Engine No. 61 stalled again after another hard push in the snow. These electric engines were powered by a catenary system consisting of an overhead trolley line and a raised power pole with a small wheel that runs along the line. The line operates at 600 volts of direct current.

Engine No. 61 has almost stalled in snow about 12 feet deep. This process can be time consuming, as the engine will again have to reverse and try again.

Picture an automobile trying to push through this deep snow. Engine No. 61 is again ramming the snow after backing up about a quarter mile.

Engine No. 61 will repeat this process again and again. The blade of the snowplow can be seen peering through the giant pile of snow. The electric motors driving this engine would be getting extremely hot.

Engine No. 61 has finally broken through the deep snow. This kind of operation is hard on the electric traction motors and gears because of the extreme heat at high amperage required to move such massive snowdrifts.

An electric interurban railroad connected Clear Lake, Iowa, and Mason City, Iowa. This line provided interchange railcar service between the steam railroads. This scene was photographed at the Emery, Iowa, terminal on a quiet Sunday afternoon in 1959. Shown is Iowa Terminal Railroad electric locomotive No. 60.

Electric engine No. 60 is shown coupled to a snowplow at Emery, Iowa. The Emery Shop housed parts and electrical systems for the Iowa Terminal Railroad. One can see the steel weights on the snowplow.

The weight of engine No. 228 is stenciled on the frame and shows 168,700 pounds. These engines operated on 600-volt direct current trolley lines and were powerful engines.

Locomotive No. 228 belonged to the Grand River Railway but was purchased by the Iowa Terminal for future use. The spare wheel sets beside the engine show the large gears that connect to the electric motors when these sets are put to use on the engines.

The steps on the front of electric locomotive No. 228 at Emery, Iowa, include a warning sign that reads, "Employees are warned not to get on foot-board when engine is approaching." These engines could run in either direction. The bold diagonal warning stripes are on each end to warn automobiles of their presence. Footboards are not shown but would be added later.

Warning signs read "Keep Out." Engine No. 228 is stored coupled to another electric engine owned by the Iowa Terminal Railroad. A work car, likely full of tools that would be used by the electric railroad employees, is shown ahead.

Southwest of Mason City, Iowa, a Chicago Great Western passenger train with two diesels units is stuck in the snow after a Northern Iowa blizzard. These diesel engines had a lot of power, but management should never have allowed them to tackle snows like this without a snowplow preceding the passenger train. (Courtesy of Bill White.)

Engine 104-C is being shoveled out by a crew of men. It is going to be a long day indeed for this lonely passenger train. (Courtesy of Bill White.)

This is a front view of engine No. 2594. The C&NW lettering for Chicago & North Western can be seen, which was cast into the engine's pilot beam when it was built. Massive castings such as this are required when any steam engine is built. It does not match the engine numbering, as engine numbers are frequently changed. The roundhouse behind the engine shows smoke coming from the number one stall, which means another engine is being readied for service. (Courtesy of Safford Lock.)

Engine No. 2594 is on the Chicago & North Western electric turntable for a high-definition shot of the right side of the engine. The hostler is peering out of the window of the turntable operation booth to be sure he has the engine in the correct position for the shot. The cover of the steam cylinder has been knocked off. Perhaps an automobile had struck the engine. The heavy bolts that actually hold the cylinder head in place are all intact, so there was no real damage to the engine itself. (Courtesy of Safford Lock.)

This photograph of a JS engine, No. 2424, was taken with an 8-by-10-inch view camera. Hostler Peely Garms sits in the fireman's seat to watch the picture taking. High-definition pictures like this were often taken by the railroads if the engine had been involved in an accident or had some other problem that needed to be documented for the Interstate Commerce Commission. (Courtesy of Safford Lock.)

The left side of engine No. 2424 was photographed here to show no damage was incurred on this side of the locomotive. After the engine was photographed, the hostler moved it off the turntable to await further instruction. (Courtesy of Safford Lock.)

A front view of engine No. 2424 shows the right front cylinder cover, replaced here at Mason City, Iowa. This is another 8-by-10-inch view camera picture in high definition. The engine is moving to have the fire cleaned before further assignment. (Courtesy of Safford Lock.)

In 1942, the Chicago, Rock Island & Pacific Railroad began running its largest steam locomotives over the Chicago Great Western tracks between Manly and Mason City, Iowa. Rock Island passenger engine No. 4061 was pulling a troop train southbound in Mason City near First Street, NW. The train was on a side track so that other traffic could pass. When the troop train began moving toward the main line, one of the rails under the engine rolled over, resulting in this massive derailment. (Courtesy of Mason City Public Library.)

Two huge Rock Island steam-powered wreckers, known as "Big Hooks," were called to lift engine No. 4061 back onto the tracks. This engine weighed 388 tons. The author was with his father, Seymour Angel, on this day when the locomotive was lifted back onto the rails. Even though he was a young boy, he still remembers the details of this impressive scene. (Courtesy of Mason City Public Library.)

Minneapolis & St. Louis steam-operated wrecker No. X771 was no longer used at Mason City, Iowa, after dieselization. The water car is an old tender from a locomotive. It was used to provide water to the wrecker boiler. (Courtesy of James L. Rueber.)

This photograph shows another Minneapolis & St. Louis steam-powered wrecker, No. X-3. This would also be referred to as a "Big Hook." In their day, these were the only machines that could lift a massive steam locomotive after a derailment or collision. (Courtesy of James L. Rueber.)

On Tuesday, February 2, 1944, during World War II, two Chicago, Milwaukee, St. Paul & Pacific locomotives, No. 802 and No. 456, collided head on at 5:25 p.m. The accident occurred 1.5 miles west of the Clear Lake, Iowa, golf course. Engine No. 802 was running as a light extra—the engine and a caboose only. This extra was being sent westbound to Sanborn, Iowa, for use at that engine terminal. Upon collision, the lighter engine, No. 802, bounced away from engine No. 456, which was pulling a train of several thousand tons. The sheer power of the collision caused the two engines to rebound from each other, landing nearly 75 feet apart. The engine crewmen all jumped to safety before the crash. Only three men were injured. S.E. Steece, the breakman on engine No. 456, received a wrist injury; Al Kleinow, the fireman of No. 802, sustained an ankle injury; and Tom Rafferty, the fireman on No. 456, incurred a hip injury. Al Kleinow's son later became the chief of police of Mason City, Iowa. (Courtesy of Safford Lock.)

Engine No. 456 was pulling eastbound freight train No. 94, as shown in this picture. The tremendous force of the collision crushed the railroad car behind the engine tender. Ralph Replogle, the Milwaukee Road traveling engineer in the leather cap, is looking at the wreckage. Ralph hired Jim Angel as a fireman several years later, in 1953. Safford Lock took these photographs in absolute darkness. Using time exposure photography, he placed his camera on a tripod and moved around the scene while pressing No. 25 flash bulbs as he walked to illuminate the black engines in the night. (Courtesy of Safford Lock.)

Engine No. 802 is shown at the Milwaukee Railroad roundhouse at Mason City, Iowa, following the accident that occurred on February 2, 1944. The cross compound air pumps and crushed cab of the locomotive can be seen. (Courtesy of Safford Lock.)

Both engines, No. 802 and No. 456, were dragged to the Mason City, Iowa, roundhouse after the accident. The two engines were shoved together to save space. These engines were never rebuilt, and they were eventually junked after 1953, when Jim Angel was hired on the Chicago, Milwaukee, St. Paul & Pacific Railroad. (Courtesy of Safford Lock.)

Pictured is a Chicago Great Western derailment in Burchinal, Iowa, on July 13, 1947. Engine No. 912 derailed and overturned while pulling a passenger train. At the time of the derailment, a road foreman was performing a track inspection. In order to get a good view of the track, the foreman was sitting in the fireman's seat on the left side of the engine. When the engine overturned, the road foreman was killed. The engineer and the fireman were not injured. (Courtesy of James L. Rueber.)

Chicago, Rock Island & Pacific steam engine No. 2581 was heading north at Mason City, Iowa, in 1947 when the engineer discovered that a switch was showing red instead of the normal green. This indicated that the train was heading into a dead-end track. The engineer put the air break into the emergency position, and when the engine finally came to a stop, it was leaning to the right against a gasoline-filled building. The engine crew was able to jump off before the locomotive came to rest. The alertness of the engineer and his quick reactions were able to prevent the engine from running straight into the building.

A dieselized passenger train and a steam-powered freight train collided head-on in this accident on the Chicago, Rock Island & Pacific Railroad at Plymouth, Iowa, around 1954. The diesel engine crew was trapped inside the cab. The local fire department had to climb on the steam engine and go into the cab through a window. The board shown atop the steam engine's smokestack had nothing to do with stopping the smoke from coming out of the engine; it was merely laid upon the stack after the firemen had used it to crawl across the top of the steam engine while rescuing the diesel crew. There were some minor injuries reported by the diesel crew, but the steam engine crew was luckily able to jump to safety before the crash.

Four

HISTORICAL PEOPLE, PLACES, AND THINGS

Author Jim Angel is standing near the pontoon bridges at Marquette, Iowa, in 1957. He spent the afternoon photographing the bridges. These pontoon bridges were used for many years to allow the Milwaukee Road to cross both spans of the Mississippi River at Marquette, Iowa.

The Milwaukee Road passenger trains reached Chicago through Marquette, Iowa, where they crossed two channels of the Mississippi River. They then went through Madison, Wisconsin, and on to Chicago, Illinois. There was no real bridge at Marquette, Iowa; instead, there were pontoon bridges that floated on the river. This photograph shows the bridge opening to let towboats pass through. A bridge tender allowed one end of the pontoon to float down the river. The other end of the pontoon bridge was hinged to the stationary portion.

After the towboats passed, the tender operated a steam engine to reel in a cable connected to the pontoon end. This would pull the pontoon back in line with the railroad. The tender would then operate machinery that would raise or lower the railroad tracks onto the pontoon. This alignment would allow the trains to pass.

Only passenger trains with light engines could cross the river. The pontoon bridge is shown aligned for normal railroad traffic. This operation proceeded daily for more than 75 years. The author spent many late afternoons here fishing with his friend and engineer Foster Merritt.

This high bridge in Fort Dodge, Iowa, spans the Des Moines River and was built in 1904. Chicago Great Western refrigerated cars are shown coming from the meat-packing plants in Fort Dodge in the 1940s. This bridge is so strong that in 2018, it still carries heavy railroad traffic for the Union Pacific. (Courtesy of James L. Rueber.)

The sign on the high bridge at Fort Dodge read "Notice—All persons are forbidden to walk over or trespass in any way upon this bridge." The c. 1910 photograph shows a mail car and three passenger cars being pulled by a steam engine. (Courtesy of James L. Rueber.)

The bridge is 220 feet high and 2,582 feet long. It was built for the Chicago Great Western Railroad. Walter P. Chrysler, of the Chrysler Building in New York City and the automotive corporation carrying his name, was the superintendent of motive power for the Chicago Great Western Railroad in Oelwein, Iowa, prior to his booming career in the automotive industry. (Courtesy of James L. Rueber.)

This is a Milwaukee Road I5 switch engine crossing the bridge over Highway 65 at Mason City, Iowa. There are 1930s-era automobiles passing underneath. The smoke is picturesque on a cold winter day. (Courtesy of Mason City Public Library.)

A joint mainline timber bridge of the Chicago Great Western and the Chicago, Rock Island & Pacific Railroads is shown across Lehigh Row in Mason City, Iowa. In 1942, after the start of World War II, bridges had to be strengthened to support the huge 4050- and 5000-class steam engines that were used to pull wartime trains. This road ran between the Northwestern States Portland Cement Plant and the Lehigh Portland Cement Plant. There were two eating and drinking establishments on the west side of Mason City, and the center post shown here was struck several times at night by passing automobile drivers. The railroad added reflective stripes in an attempt to make the post more visible, but problems continued until its removal after the dieselization of the Rock Island. (Courtesy of Mason City Public Library.)

William Howard Taft is visiting Mason City, Iowa, at the Milwaukee Road depot on September 26, 1908. This photograph was captured while he was campaigning to be elected president. (Courtesy of Mason City Public Library.)

Alf Landon visited Mason City in June 1936 while campaigning against Franklin D. Roosevelt in the presidential election. His campaign train is shown at the joint Chicago Great Western and Chicago, Rock Island & Pacific passenger depot. The large crowd gathered around the last car on the train to hear the campaign speech. (Courtesy of Mason City Public Library.)

A D-class fast mail train, engine No. 1443 of the Chicago & North Western, is shown in 1918 at the Eagle Grove, Iowa, train station. This locomotive was capable of speeds up to 100 miles per hour on the Chicago & North Western main line. The class D engine drive wheels were 81 inches in diameter, which was very large for this period. These engines were built between 1900 and 1908. (Courtesy of Mason City Public Library.)

Minneapolis & St. Louis switch engine No. 66 is shown at the Mason City depot. This photograph was taken through the window of the passenger depot. A portion of the engine is blocked by the telegraph sounder that sat on a desk within the depot. (Courtesy of Mason City Public Library.)

This is a c. 1910 photograph taken at the Chicago & North Western depot in Mason City, Iowa. A small A-class passenger engine with a mail car and two passenger cars made of wood are sitting in front of the depot. Wooden cars were standard for this era. Railroads carried all of the mail for many, many years until the US Postal Service switched all of the mail to trucks. (Courtesy of Mason City Public Library.)

Passenger service had ceased at the Chicago & North Western passenger depot at Mason City, Iowa in the 1950s. The train dispatchers were housed on the second floor. All train dispatching was soon moved to Boone, Iowa. (Courtesy of Elwin Musser.)

This vacant Chicago & North Western depot was photographed in Mason City, Iowa, in the mid-1950s. This building was no longer in service and was eventually torn down.

This photograph is looking to the west at the joint Chicago, Rock Island, & Pacific and Chicago Great Western passenger depot in Mason City, Iowa. There are two parked automobiles, which appear to be mid-1930s Ford and Plymouth models, in the depot lot. The two railroads jointly operated over the Chicago Great Western–owned tracks between Clear Lake Junction and Manly, Iowa, a distance of about nine miles. (Courtesy of Mason City Public Library.)

The Chicago, Rock Island, & Pacific and Chicago Great Western depot is shown during the diesel age with a passenger train stopped at the depot. Passenger baggage is being loaded into the baggage car. Passengers are boarding at the front of the train.

This engine belonged to the Chicago, Milwaukee & St. Paul Railroad at this point in time, before the line extended to the West Coast; the railroad later added Pacific to its name. Engine No. 221 is pulling a "Business Men's Special" of six passenger cars from Lawler, Iowa, to Mason City in 1909. (Courtesy of Mason City Public Library.)

Engine No. 221 has arrived at the Mason City, Iowa, roundhouse in 1909 with the Business Men's Special. This photograph is extremely sharp and was probably taken with a view camera that provided an 8-by-10-inch negative. The author was unable to identify any of the engine crew. When the author first started firing for the Milwaukee Road, he knew of only two engineers who would have had the seniority to be able to recognize any of these three engine men. One engineer was Lou Walter, with a service date of 1907. The other was "Buttermilk" Peterson, whose service date was 1904. Of course, the engine men are no longer around to help with identification. (Courtesy of James L. Rueber.)

The Milwaukee Road depot at Mason City, Iowa, was built around 1870 and fielded the first passenger train into Mason City on the Chicago, Milwaukee, St. Paul & Pacific Railroad. Passenger operation lasted from 1870 until passenger train No. 22, *The Sioux*, was discontinued after 90 years of service in 1960. (Courtesy of Mason City Public Library.)

This is an interior view of the east side of the old passenger depot in Mason City, likely taken prior to the end of World War I in 1918. A poster hanging on the depot wall reads "United For Victory," which is indicative of this era. This depot still stands in 2018. At one time, there was a lunchroom were passengers could stop in for a quick meal while the steam engines were being changed to a fresh engine along their journey. (Courtesy of Mason City Public Library.)

The west side of the passenger depot shows more of where passengers would await their trains. There is a penny-operated scale in the corner. These scales were common in depots and provided passengers with something simple to pass the time while waiting for their trains to arrive. The Chicago, Milwaukee, St. Paul & Pacific Railroad map is displayed on the wall for passengers to study. (Courtesy of Mason City Public Library.)

This an aerial view of the massive Milwaukee Road roundhouse and switching yards in Mason City, Iowa, in 1946. The roundhouse consisted of 21 stalls and feasibly employed up to 200 men. This roundhouse was capable of rebuilding steam locomotives, replacing wheels, and all boiler work and other heavy machine work. (Courtesy of Mason City Public Library.)

Another view of the Milwaukee Road roundhouse looking north shows the passenger depot on the left. The water tank and the house boilers are also seen across from the depot. The house boilers provided steam to passenger cars in the wintertime, and they could be used to raise steam quickly for steam locomotives that had to be used on short notice. (Courtesy of Mason City Public Library.)

John Ficken and one of his sons are photographed at the Chicago & North Western Railroad roundhouse at Mason City, Iowa. The five stalls house an M2-class switch engine, an R1 light freight engine, and a passenger motorcar. Each of these engines was being serviced on a quiet Sunday morning with the electric turntable in position. The Chicago & North Western had a large 16-stall roundhouse in use into the 1930s. With the introduction of bigger engines, fewer engines were actually needed, which in turn reduced the need for large roundhouses. This roundhouse was reduced to five stalls in 1946.

The first five stalls of the Milwaukee Road roundhouse are shown around 1910. The roundhouse was later built out to 21 stalls. The first three stalls were turned into engine crew rooms, which included bathrooms with shower stalls. The dirty engine men could clean up in the roundhouse before their next run or before heading home at the end of their shift. (Courtesy of Mason City Public Library.)

The southeastern end of the 21-stall Milwaukee Road roundhouse is pictured. When the roundhouse was expanded, large picnic tables were placed inside to provide a place for each engine crew to meet to discuss its incoming and outgoing runs. This was called the crew room. (Courtesy of Mason City Public Library.)

The electric turntables were on the eastern end of the Milwaukee roundhouse. Turntables were used to move the engines onto the proper track or into the proper stalls, and to turn locomotives around. Engines were not backed into the stalls; they always entered head first, facing in a westerly direction. If the engine were to be used on a train going east, the engine had to be rotated on the turntable so that it was facing east.

Roundhouses were always dark and gloomy, especially at night. These F5-class locomotives, No. 817 and No. 825, were photographed at the Milwaukee Road roundhouse. (Courtesy of Safford Lock.)

This cameraman is having some fun with another photographer's camera. A 4-by-5-inch speed graphic camera is flippantly being adjusted with a large wrench that was normally used on steam locomotives. This night shot was captured in the Milwaukee Road roundhouse in Mason City. (Courtesy of Safford Lock.)

DIESELIZED SINCE 1952, THE MODERN ROCK ISLAND SALUTES A MEMORY.

This Christmas card is courtesy of the Rock Island Railroad. This was sent by J.S. Caroll, an employee of the Rock Island, to Seymour Angel of the Chicago & North Western Railroad in 1952 to celebrate the dieselization of the Chicago, Rock Island & Pacific Railroad. Railroad artist Howard Fogg illustrated this holiday card. Fogg did many illustrations of railroad scenes, locomotives, and landscapes.

The iron horse has undergone many changes since the Rock Island celebrated its first Christmas, 105 years ago. But there's one thing we will never change — the sincere desire that you enjoy a memorable Holiday Season followed by a year of rich fulfillment.

Rock Island

Seymour Angel, the author's father, worked at this old Mason City telegraph station for 38 years. This switchmen's shanty is shown in 1962 before being completely torn down. This office was used by the Chicago & North Western telegraphers and switchmen for many years.

Seymour Angel was photographed at the key in Mason City, Iowa, on the evening of his retirement in 1957. Seymour was born in Heart's Content, Newfoundland, Canada, where the giant cable ship *Great Eastern* landed the first undersea telegraph cables across the Atlantic Ocean from England to the North American continent. Here is where he learned telegraphy. Seymour went to work for Western Union in Chicago and served in the American Army during World War I. Western Union had promised that workers would return to jobs after the war, but it reneged on these promises. Still in uniform, he stood forlornly on the steps of the Western Union building when a man walked up to him and said, "Hey buddy, can you telegraph?" He was then offered a telegrapher's job in Mason City in 1919, and he lived and worked there until 1957. (Courtesy of Elwin Musser.)

A close-up shows Seymour Angel's hand on a telegraph key known as a Vibraplex Bug. It took a real expert telegrapher to use these keys at high speeds. All railroads used the telegraph, because in those days there was no rural electricity and very little telephone service to all of the railroad depots. Telegraphy was a reliable way of communication, since the railroads provided their own poles and wires along the tracks. (Courtesy of Elwin Musser.)

This photograph was taken at the Milwaukee Railroad depot at Mason City on November 29, 1943. Mrs. Seymour Angel, the general chair of the committees from the First Christian Church, reported that over 500 servicemen were served coffee and donuts over Thanksgiving Weekend. The First Christian Church committees were headed by Mildred Bailey, Mrs. Leo Allstot, Mrs. Dewey Paul, Mrs. Oliver Ong, Mrs. Ray Crispin, and Mrs. Richard Humiston. Each evening, about two hours prior to the arrival of train No. 22 from the west, the conductor on the train would count all of the servicemen and wire the total to Mason City so that the women would know how much coffee and donuts to prepare. The food was all handmade. Capt. Perry Stamp heads the line of servicemen, and the women serving them from left to right are Mrs. Jack Griffith, Evelyn Barness, Anna Hoveland, Mrs. Rogness, Mrs. Herman Peterson, and Mrs. Harold Randall (pouring the coffee). Mrs. Hoyt Gaarder is not shown but also served on the committee. The train stopped at the Mason City station at 9:30 p.m. so that the engine could be changed and left the station at 9:50 p.m. All servicemen were served in 20 minutes. The servicemen loved it and always left giving their thanks to all who could hear. It must be remembered that not all the servicemen returned from this most horrible war. (Courtesy of Safford Lock.)

Five

COMING OF A NEW ERA WITH DIESEL LOCOMOTIVES

Engine No. 457 spent many years running the nightly Armour Packing Company meat train from Mason City to Ackley, Iowa. The cars would be picked up by the Illinois Central for a fast run to Chicago. After retirement from the Minneapolis & St. Louis Railway, this engine worked every fall at the Mason City plant of American Crystal Sugar. The engine was watched over by the Minneapolis & St. Louis roundhouse foreman, Eric Darwitz. This engine was one of the last great steam engines before the coming of diesel. (Courtesy of James L. Rueber.)

Minneapolis & St. Louis engine No. 457 is in the process of being moved to its permanent resting place at East Park in Mason City, Iowa. Before moving to East Park, engine No. 457 was cleaned up at the Chicago, Milwaukee, St. Paul & Pacific roundhouse. It was moved up the Austin branch tracks of the Milwaukee Road. Temporary track was laid into East Park to move this engine into place. Milwaukee Road traveling engineer Ralph Replogle sat in the engineer's seat to control the compressed air that was piped to the engine for braking power if required. The engine derailed once and had to be re-railed with additional pulling power provided by the Caterpillar tractor alongside the engine.

Engine No. 457 was placed at East Park in 1957. The fence was installed around the engine to protect it from vandals. The storm curtains are visible in the cab. There is little to no protection from the elements at this point in time.

This later view of engine No. 457 is shown without the storm curtains. Vandals had stolen these curtains, several gauges from inside the cab, the whistle, and other removable items from the locomotive. Graffiti covered the engine number, and it became apparent that something needed to be done to keep this piece of history from being reduced to rusty junk. The park installed a security light in an effort to deter vandals, but this effort was futile.

Volunteers decided to work as a group to cosmetically restore this great engine. They wanted to bring it back to the appearance it had when it was working on the Minneapolis & St. Louis Railway. This effort required railfans all across Iowa to come together and help locate missing parts and pieces. Many talented people collaborated on this project to ensure that it was historically accurate. This engine had been stripped of its boiler lagging, and cosmetic work was done with replacement materials to simulate this. New sheet metal was used to cover these materials and bring back the appearance of the original boiler. While this engine has been cosmetically restored, it could likely never run again, as the cost of replacing the boiler, all piping, tubes, and flues within, and all other operative parts would be prohibitively high. (Courtesy of Owen Currier.)

During the cosmetic restoration, restorers worked to give a reasonable facsimile of the inside of a steam engine cab. The handiwork of the restorers is evident where steam gauges, water gauges, and air gauges were installed to show what a back head, or the back end of a boiler, looked like to the engine men who operated these locomotives. (Courtesy of Owen Currier.)

The lower half of the back head showcases the butterfly fire doors in the open position. The fireman opened these doors by stepping on a foot pedal, which allowed him to easily check the condition of the fire. The restoration of this locomotive fills the city park commission with pride because of a job so ably done. As it now sits under cover from the elements, many visitors will be able to enjoy the beauty of steam. (Courtesy of Owen Currier.)

This 1,000-horsepower diesel switch engine was acquired in the 1940s at the Chicago & North Western yard in Mason City, Iowa. Shown are the engine men, switchmen, and roundhouse man. These engines were extremely powerful and only required diesel fuel at crew changes. They worked around the clock, eliminating many M2 steam switch engines, which had to have fires cleaned every eight hours. The M2 engines also required additional maintenance, such as greasing main and side rods. This was the beauty of diesel. Crew changes still had to be made every eight hours, as people, unlike diesel engines, could not work around the clock. (Courtesy of Elwin Musser.)

Minneapolis & St. Louis Railway switcher No. 218 stands at the new roundhouse. The old five-stall steam engine roundhouse was struck by lightning shortly after World War II and had to be torn down. As steam engines were still in use until 1950, this roundhouse was designed to handle both steam and diesel locomotives. It had two smokejacks in the north end of the roundhouse roof for steam and ventilators in the south end for diesel.

After the Chicago & North Western Railway bought out the Minneapolis & St. Louis, the engines carried the Chicago & North Western name. The numbering, as indicated on engines No. 255 and No. 212, remained the same.

The air-operated turntable remained in service until the Minneapolis & St. Louis facility was eliminated. Steam locomotives used this turntable for many years before the diesels replaced steam in 1950. This photograph was taken in 1957.

Hostler John Ficken is standing on engine No. 212. John had two jobs following the acquisition of the Minneapolis & St. Louis Railway by the Chicago & North Western Railway. He started his day working on the old Minneapolis & St. Louis engines. After finishing here, he would go across town to the Chicago & North Western roundhouse to finish his day. All of these engines still utilized the large bells that were taken from the retired steam engines.

This passenger locomotive standing at the Chicago & North Western depot in Mason City was used by many railroad branch lines starting in the 1920s. They were powered by gasoline or oil engines and were cheaper to operate than steam engines because they required only one engineer. They were usually called "Doodlebugs" because of the gaudy cross hatch of colors on the front of the engine to alert motorists of their oncoming presence. They used what was called a "dead man's pedal" because there was only one person in the cab. The engineer had to keep his foot on this pedal when running the engine. If something happened and his foot came off the pedal, the engine would stop automatically. (Courtesy of Elwin Musser.)

This 1947 photograph shows a similar Doodlebug on the Minneapolis & St. Louis Railway bridge at Mason City, Iowa. The author of this book is shown standing next to his uncle Glenn Scott watching the first train passing over the completed bridge. The operator can be seen in the picture. These trains carried passengers, mail, creamery products, and other short-haul station commodities. These engines also were operated by one engineer and utilized the dead man's pedal. (Courtesy of Elwin Musser.)

Milwaukee Road passenger engine No. 804 is on standby at Mason City for use in case one of the diesel units on freight train No. 62 should fail. The steam engine would be added to the train so that speed could be maintained up the hill from Fort Atkinson to Calmer, Iowa. The steam engine would then be removed at Calmer. (Courtesy of Milwaukee Public Library.)

This photograph is of a trial passenger motorcar on the Milwaukee Road at Mason City. Motorcars were driven by different types of engines. The Chicago & North Western utilized gasoline-powered engines, while the Minneapolis & St. Louis utilized kerosene engines. This particular motor was not a success for the Milwaukee, so it reverted to steam engines. (Courtesy of Mason City Public Library.)

The advent of diesel on the Milwaukee Road arrived in 1947 at Mason City, Iowa. Engine No. 82A heads a locomotive of three diesel units. These new engines meant the demise of the steam engines over the next few years. Louis Hansen was a Mason City fireman and engineer. He is being congratulated for his last run of service in 1952. Pictured from left to right are roundhouse foreman Paul Hurley, traveling engineer Ralph Replogle, Louis Hansen, assistant superintendent R.W. Graves, Ed Walter, H. Milnes, and Lou Walter. The author personally knew some of these men, who were senior engineers and officials. Ralph Replogle is the traveling engineer who hired the author in 1953 on the Milwaukee Road. Lou Walter, the tall man on the right, had a service date of 1907. These old heads knew they had the seniority to hold down the jobs on these engines.

Engine No. 86A was another new diesel locomotive consisting of three units. These new engines were child's play for the old steam engineers to run. They had heated cabs and comfortable seats. The noise of the steam engines, which caused many old engineers to lose some of their hearing, no longer existed on these diesel locomotives. The EMD (Electro Motive Division of General Motors Corporation) contained a diesel two-cycle V16 engine that generated a combined total of over 4,000 horsepower. The diesels had a wonderful feature called dynamic braking. In the steam days, train No. 62 would bring all of the refrigerator cars from the Sioux Falls, South Dakota, packinghouses. They would travel over Monona Hill to Marquette, Iowa, making heavy usage of the train's air brakes. This could cause fire and sparks to encircle the car wheels, and wrecks were possible due to overheated axles and wheel bearings. By moving a lever in the cab, the engineer could put the diesel locomotive into dynamic braking. This changed the electric motors on the engine from using electricity to generating electricity, which was dissipated into the electrical grid on the top of the locomotive and provided powerful braking of the train without any use of the air brakes. The brake shoes were not needed down the hill, resulting in no sparks and no fires descending the hill.

Ed Walter (left) had 57 years of engine service, and his brother Lou Walter (right) had 60 years of engine service on the Chicago, Milwaukee, St. Paul & Pacific Railroad at Mason City, Iowa, when they both retired at the end of August 1963. Their youngest brother, Harry Walter, who was also in engine service, died before their retirement. Railroading has been a family occupation for many years and continues to be today. (Courtesy of Elwin Musser.)

Lou Walter was an oddity in his day. He excelled in the art of crocheting. He is posing here for a photograph while in his daily railroad clothes. He is crocheting in the yard master's switch shanty at Mason City with Ralph Joint, the Mason City yard master. (Courtesy of Elwin Musser.)

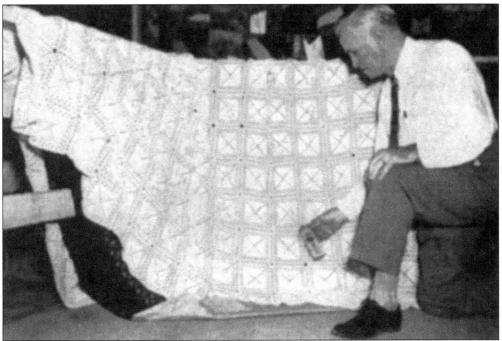

Lou Walter's "railroad hands" won him first place in the 1948 national needlework contest. His crocheted bedspread was the best of the works submitted by nearly 700 men. The lace-like spread was 102 inches long and 80 inches wide. (Courtesy of Elwin Musser.)

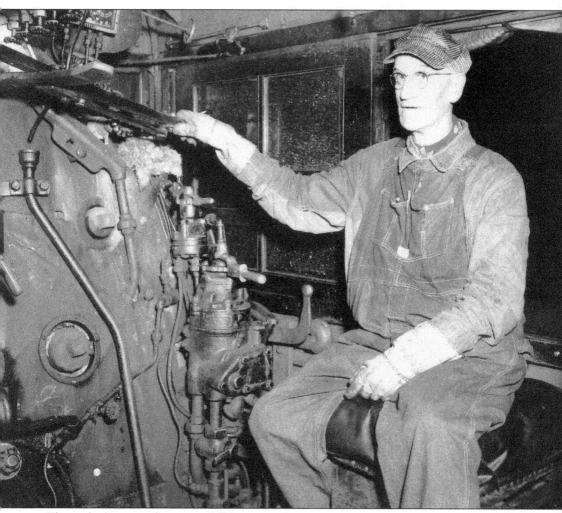

This is the last run of engineer Bill Barr upon his retirement as engineer on passenger train No. 22 on the Milwaukee Road at Mason City, Iowa. Note the typical garb of an engine man: gauntlet gloves were worn to protect the hands and forearms, neckerchiefs kept hot cinders from getting under the collar, and a wad of waste was handy near the throttle. This was surely not the dinner party typical of most retirements today. (Courtesy of Safford Lock.)

Engineer Charlie Crepow stands next to his wife and an unidentified gentleman in front of engine No. 810 at the Milwaukee Road depot in Mason City. This would be Charlie's last trip before his retirement. He has just finished oiling around the engine, as he is shown holding the long-necked oil can in his hand. The cameraman has formatted a nice photograph with friends watching. A 1930s automobile is shown in the middle background, and a 1920s car is on the right side of the photograph. (Courtesy of Safford Lock.)

Ellen Crepow is waving to her husband in Engine No. 810 as he begins to roll east toward Marquette, Iowa, with the passenger train. Mrs. Crepow's overshoes were the style in the 1930s. When World War II began a few years later, all rubber was rationed, so hopefully she hung onto her precious footwear! (Courtesy of Safford Lock.)

Another Milwaukee Road engineer is retiring and stepping down off engine No. 802. Goggles were often worn by engineers and firemen, depending upon which way the wind was blowing. A young fireman looks on as officials stand looking at the retirement papers before handing them to the new retiree. Many of the officials and engineers in this scene have 40-plus years of service with the railroad. (Courtesy of Safford Lock.)

Engineer Bill Blackmarr is at the throttle of a new diesel switch engine on the Milwaukee Road at Mason City, Iowa. The old engineers still dressed much like they did when running steam engines. Gauntlet gloves and neckerchiefs were not really necessary, because there was not any soot or hot cinders present in the relatively clean diesel cabs. (Courtesy of Elwin Musser.)

Art Holtman retired as the press room foreman at the *Mason City Globe Gazette* newspaper. He is posing by Engine No. 133C on a Sunday afternoon at the Milwaukee Road roundhouse at Mason City.

Holtman took time to photograph the engines awaiting assignment on Monday morning to train No. 62 from Mason City, Iowa, to Sioux Falls, South Dakota. Art was a dear friend of author Jim Angel.

A new diesel locomotive of the Chicago, Rock Island & Pacific Railroad is approaching the Rock Island–Chicago Great Western depot at Mason City. These trains were known as "Rockets" and were the newest thing in passenger travel in 1939. They were capable of speeds over 90 miles per hour. (Courtesy of Mason City Public Library.)

The Rock Island Railroad was one of the first in Mason City to use the new streamlined electromotive diesel locomotives for fast passenger trains between Des Moines, Iowa, and Minneapolis, Minnesota. These diesel locomotives were manufactured by the Electro Motive Division of General Motors. They were clean, smoke free, and extremely fast, thus giving them the "Rocket" name. On October 22, 1937, one of these Rockets struck a school bus coming from Renwick, Iowa, killing seven students, two teachers, and the bus driver. There was always a question as to whether the bus driver confused the diesel horn with the old steam locomotive chime whistle. (Courtesy of Mason City Public Library.)

This Rock Island Rocket was photographed at Mason City, Iowa, in the late 1940s. The water tank and water spout are still in evidence, signaling that some steam engines are still in use. An old Packard automobile is in the foreground. (Courtesy of Mason City Public Library.)

Jim Angel fired steam locomotives on both the Milwaukee Road and the Chicago & North Western. He was loaned from the Milwaukee Road to the Chicago & North Western Railroad to perform duties on both lines. He had to have two switch keys to perform his duties. The Chicago & North Western switch key would open any lock on the North Iowa Division of the Chicago & North Western Railway. The Chicago, Milwaukee, St. Paul & Pacific switch key would open any lock on the Iowa Dakota Division of the Milwaukee Road.

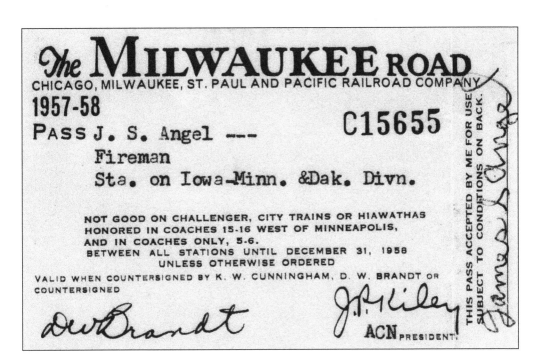

This 1957–1958 Milwaukee Road employee pass belonged to fireman Jim Angel. He could use this pass to ride any Milwaukee passenger train on the Iowa Dakota Division to get to any location that he needed so that he could perform his job.

NOT GOOD IN SUBURBAN TERRITORY, BETWEEN
CHICAGO, ELGIN AND WALWORTH.

CONDITIONS

The person accepting and using this pass thereby assumes all risk of accident and injury to person, and all damage to or loss of property. If presented by any other than the individual named thereon, Conductor will take up pass and collect fare. As a condition precedent to the issue and use of this pass, the recipient represents that he or she is not prohibited by Federal or State laws from receiving free transportation, and that this pass will be lawfully used.

NOT TRANSFERABLE

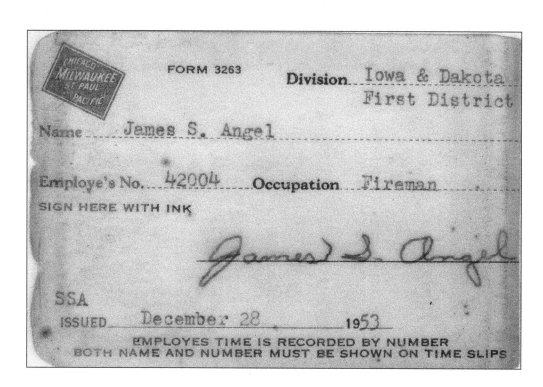

Jim Angel's seniority date was established on December 28, 1953. This card was to be carried at all times by employees of the Chicago, Milwaukee, St. Paul & Pacific Railroad to verify their starting date.

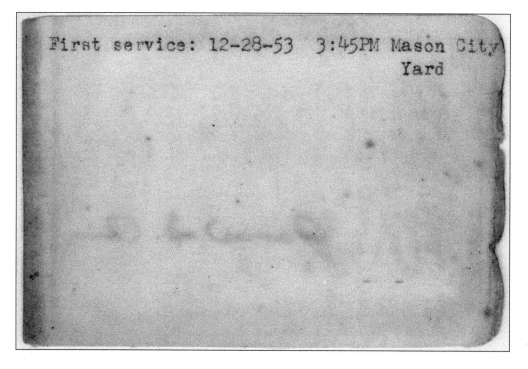

Author Jim Angel is on the *Nebraska Zephyr* with his daughter Cathy Angel, along with William Kratville and his son. Kratville was a noted railroad writer and is pictured enjoying a Sunday ride between Omaha and Lincoln, Nebraska.

This photograph was taken between Mason City and Algona, Iowa, on the Milwaukee Road in 1980. The bumper corn crop has been put on the ground, as there was not enough room in the storage bins to hold the supply produced by the fertile Iowa soil.

Retired Chicago & North Western employees are enjoying a Sunday potluck dinner at Clear Lake, Iowa, in the 1940s after World War II. Railroad officials are helping to organize the meal. The author requests assistance in naming any of the people shown in this photograph. (Courtesy of Elwin Musser.)

The Chicago & North Western roundhouse sits nearly empty in the age of the diesels. Until the building was torn down, it could be used to get diesel locomotives out of the bitterly cold Iowa conditions. Some light maintenance, such as brake shoe replacement, could be done by maintenance men, but ultimately, this roundhouse became obsolete.

The empty Chicago & North Western roundhouse at Mason City, Iowa, is awaiting demolition in the late 1950s. The diesels have overcome, and steam is a vision of the past.

Visit us at
arcadiapublishing.com

CPSIA information can be obtained
at www.ICGtesting.com
Printed in the USA
LVHW071258171221
706477LV00031B/649